How to Reproduce The Pages for Mul

he

Trace inside the big letters by following the numbers.

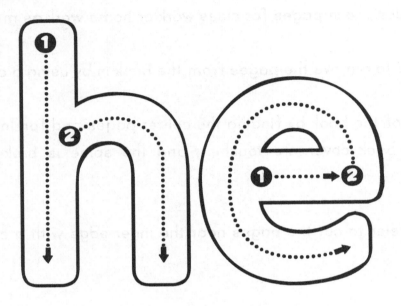

Trace the word until you are finished.

he   he   he   he

he   he   he   he

Write the word.

**the**

Trace inside the big letters by following the numbers.

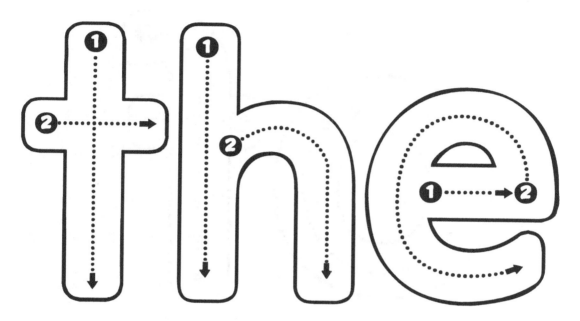

Trace the word until you are finished.

the the the the

the the the the

Write the word.

Trace inside the big letters by following the numbers.

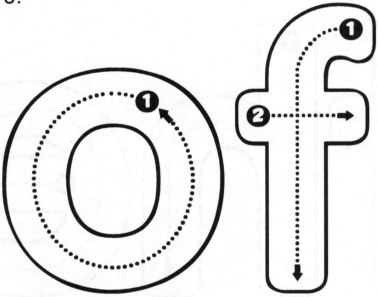

Trace the word until you are finished.

of of of of of of of

of of of of of of of

Write the word.

Trace inside the big letters by following the numbers.

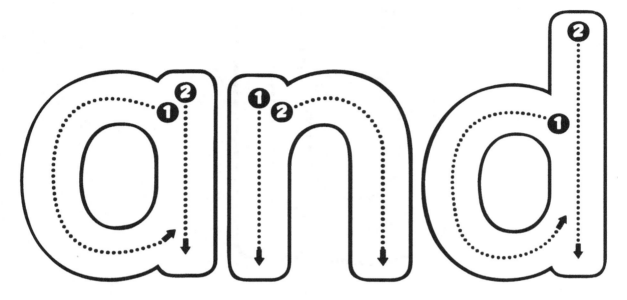

Trace the word until you are finished.

and and and

and and and

Write the word.

a

Trace inside the big letters by following the numbers.

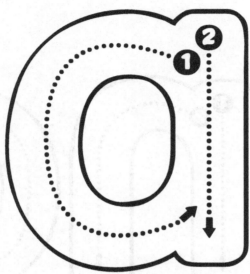

Trace the word until you are finished.

a   a   a   a   a   a

a   a   a   a   a   a

Write the word.

to

Trace inside the big letters by following the numbers.

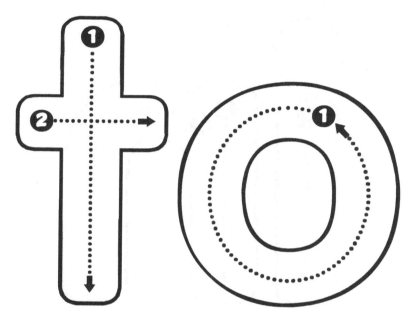

Trace the word until you are finished.

to   to   to   to   to

to   to   to   to   to

Write the word.

in

Trace inside the big letters by following the numbers.

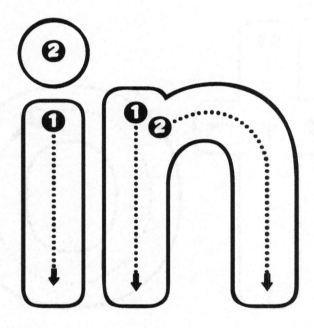

Trace the word until you are finished.

in in in in in

in in in in in

Write the word.

is

Name:..............................

Trace inside the big letters by following the numbers.

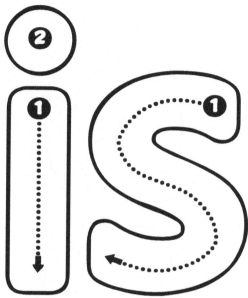

Trace the word until you are finished.

is   is   is   is   is

is   is   is   is   is

Write the word.

you

Trace inside the big letters by following the numbers.

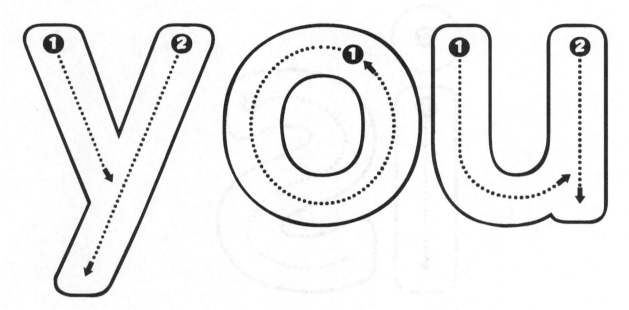

Trace the word until you are finished.

you you you

you you you

Write the word.

Trace inside the big letters by following the numbers.

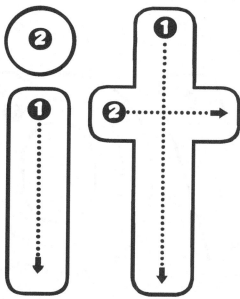

Trace the word until you are finished.

it   it   it   it   it

it   it   it   it   it

Write the word.

Trace inside the big letters by following the numbers.

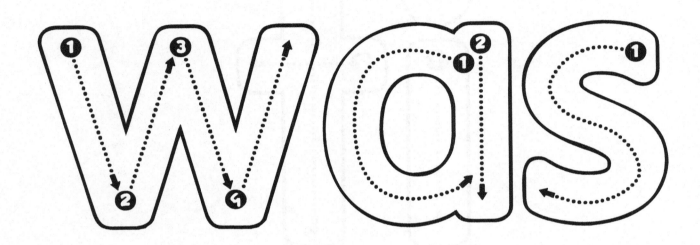

Trace the word until you are finished.

was   was   was

was   was   was

Write the word.

Trace inside the big letters by following the numbers.

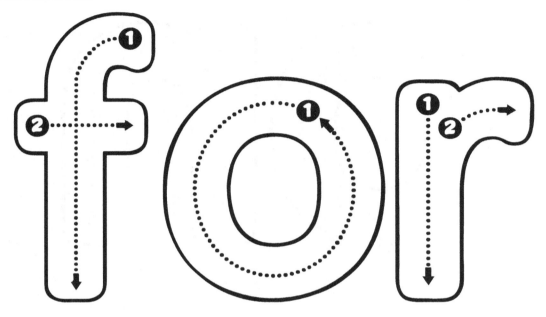

Trace the word until you are finished.

for for for for
for for for for

Write the word.

Trace inside the big letters by following the numbers.

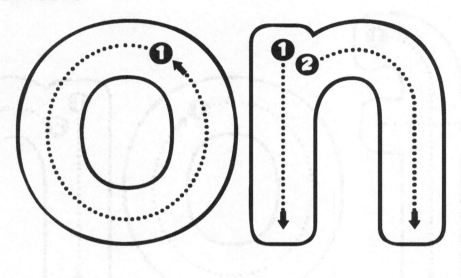

Trace the word until you are finished.

on on on on

on on on on

Write the word.

 **are**

Trace inside the big letters by following the numbers.

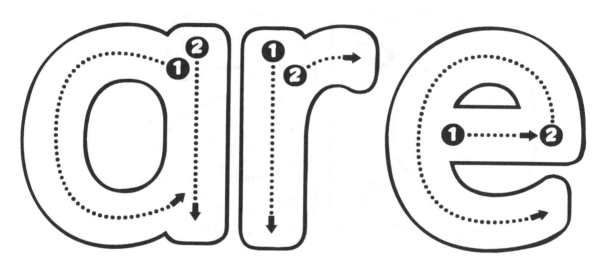

Trace the word until you are finished.

are   are   are   are

are   are   are   are

Write the word.

as

Trace inside the big letters by following the numbers.

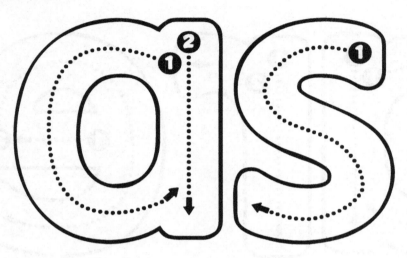

Trace the word until you are finished.

as   as   as   as

as   as   as   as

Write the word.

 **his**

Trace inside the big letters by following the numbers.

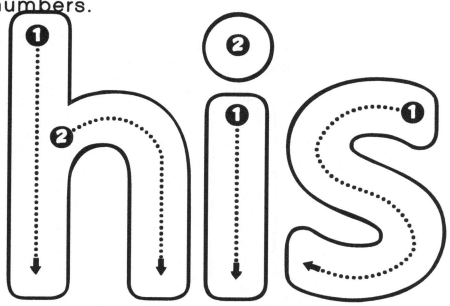

Trace the word until you are finished.

his his his his

his his his his

Write the word.

I

Trace inside the big letters by following the numbers.

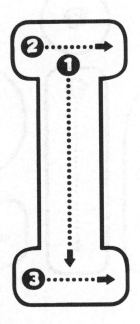

Trace the word until you are finished.

I   I   I   I   I

I   I   I   I   I

Write the word.

at

Trace inside the big letters by following the numbers.

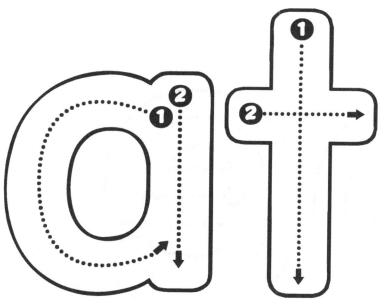

Trace the word until you are finished.

at at at at at

at at at at at

Write the word.

be

Trace inside the big letters by following the numbers.

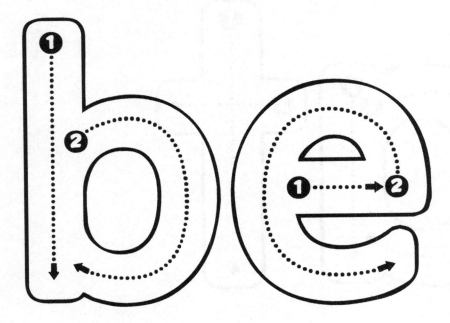

Trace the word until you are finished.

be   be   be   be

be   be   be

Write the word.

Trace inside the big letters by following the numbers.

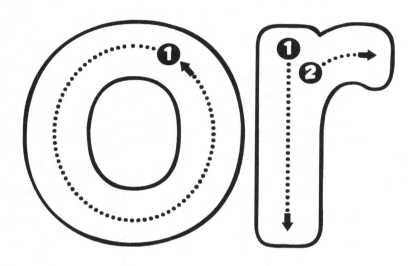

Trace the word until you are finished.

or   or   or   or   or   or

or   or   or   or   or

Write the word.

Trace inside the big letters by following the numbers.

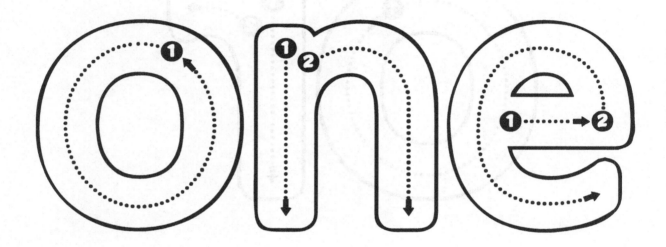

Trace the word until you are finished.

one one one one

one one one one

Write the word.

had

Trace inside the big letters by following the numbers.

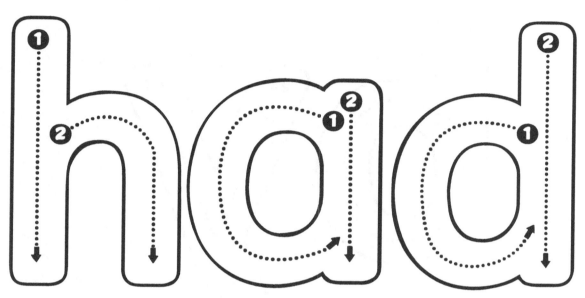

Trace the word until you are finished.

had had had

had had had

Write the word.

by

Trace inside the big letters by following the numbers.

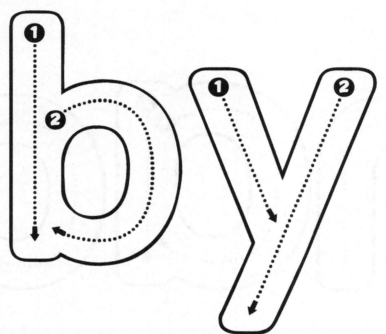

Trace the word until you are finished.

by   by   by   by   by

by   by   by   by   by

Write the word.

Trace inside the big letters by following the numbers.

Trace the word until you are finished.

but but but but

but but but but

Write the word.

not

Trace inside the big letters by following the numbers.

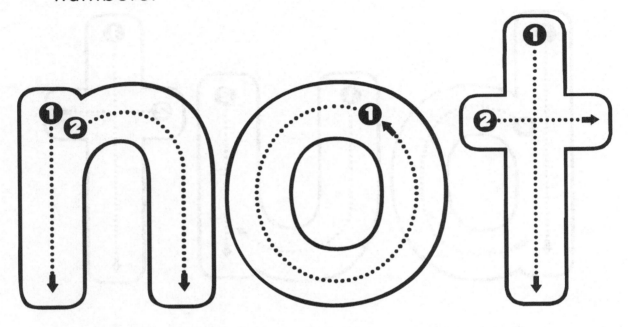

Trace the word until you are finished.

not not not not

not not not not

Write the word.

Trace inside the big letters by following the numbers.

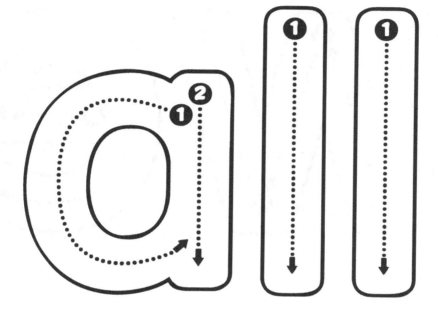

Trace the word until you are finished.

all all all all

all all all all

Write the word.

Trace inside the big letters by following the numbers.

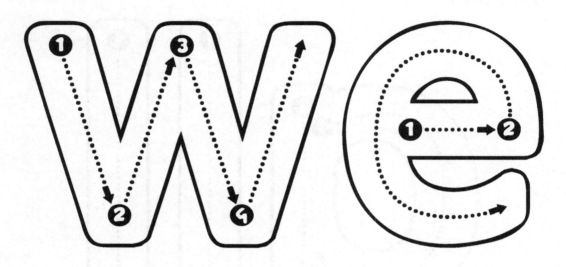

Trace the word until you are finished.

we   we   we   we

we   we   we   we

Write the word.

Trace inside the big letters by following the numbers.

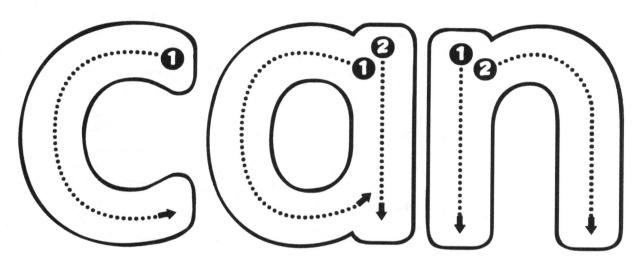

Trace the word until you are finished.

can can can

can can can

Write the word.

Trace inside the big letters by following the numbers.

Trace the word until you are finished.

use use use use

use use use use

Write the word.

an

Trace inside the big letters by following the numbers.

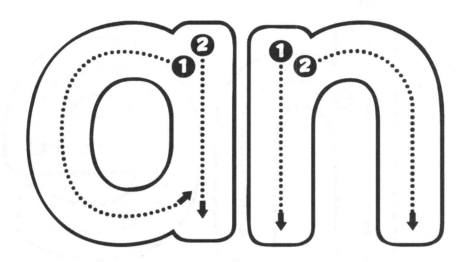

Trace the word until you are finished.

an   an   an   an

an   an   an   an

Write the word.

she

Trace inside the big letters by following the numbers.

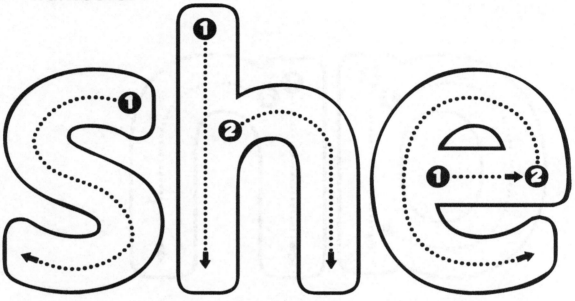

Trace the word until you are finished.

she she she

she she she

Write the word.

do

Trace inside the big letters by following the numbers.

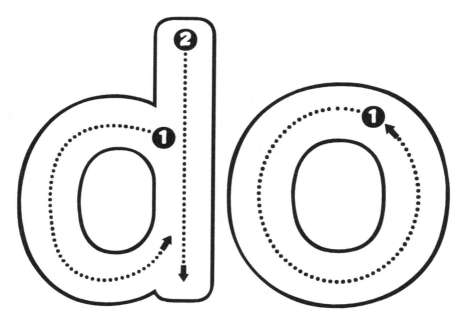

Trace the word until you are finished.

do   do   do   do

do   do   do   do

Write the word.

how

Trace inside the big letters by following the numbers.

Trace the word until you are finished.

how how how

how how how

Write the word.

Trace inside the big letters by following the numbers.

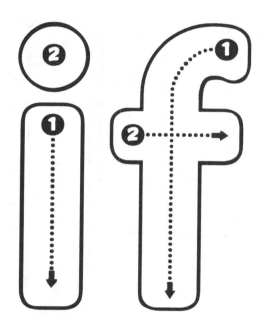

Trace the word until you are finished.

if if if if if

if if if if if

Write the word.

Trace inside the big letters by following the numbers.

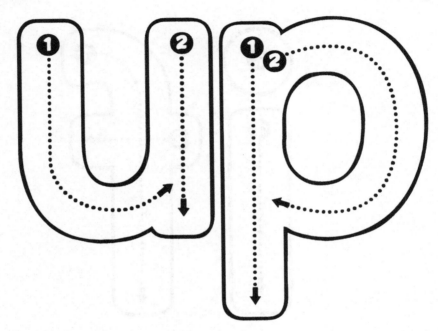

Trace the word until you are finished.

up   up   up   up

up   up   up   up

Write the word.

out

Trace inside the big letters by following the numbers.

Trace the word until you are finished.

out out out out

out out out out

Write the word.

SO

Trace inside the big letters by following the numbers.

Trace the word until you are finished.

SO   SO   SO   SO

SO   SO   SO   SO

Write the word.

her

Trace inside the big letters by following the numbers.

Trace the word until you are finished.

her her her

her her her

Write the word.

Trace inside the big letters by following the numbers.

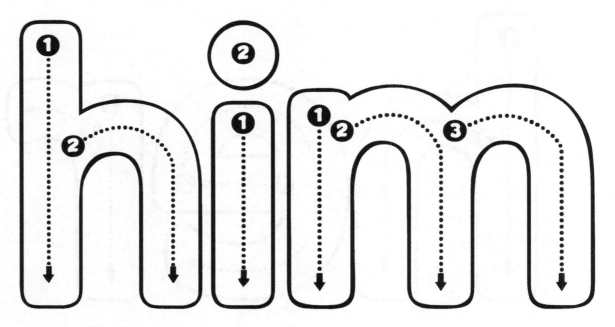

Trace the word until you are finished.

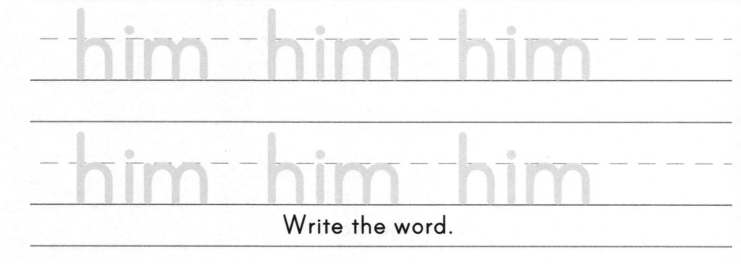

Write the word.

has

Trace inside the big letters by following the numbers.

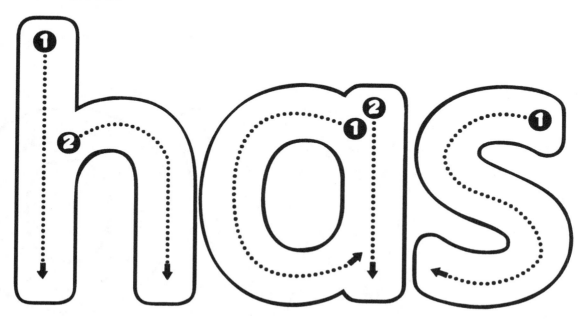

Trace the word until you are finished.

has has has

has has has

Write the word.

two

Trace inside the big letters by following the numbers.

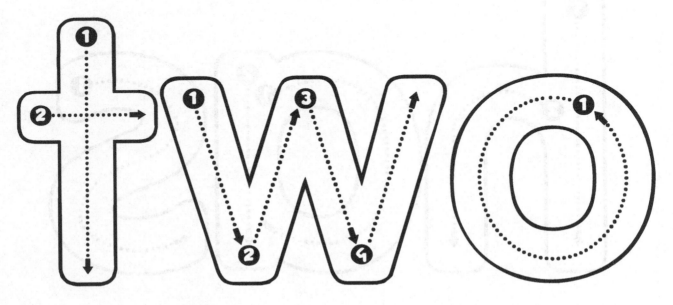

Trace the word until you are finished.

two two two

two two two

Write the word.

Trace inside the big letters by following the numbers.

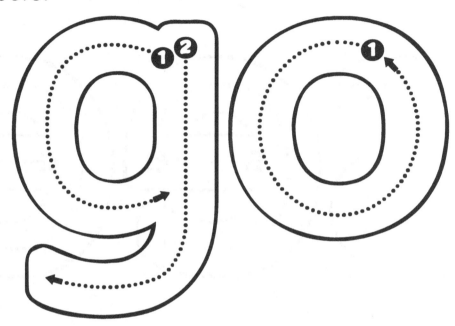

Trace the word until you are finished.

go   go   go   go

go   go   go   go

Write the word.

Trace inside the big letters by following the numbers.

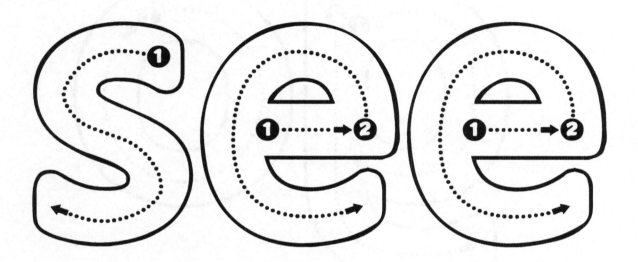

Trace the word until you are finished.

see see see

see see see

Write the word.

Trace inside the big letters by following the numbers.

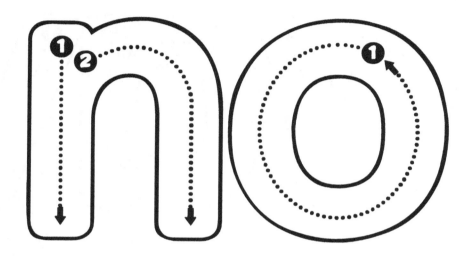

Trace the word until you are finished.

no no no no

no no no no

Write the word.

Trace inside the big letters by following the numbers.

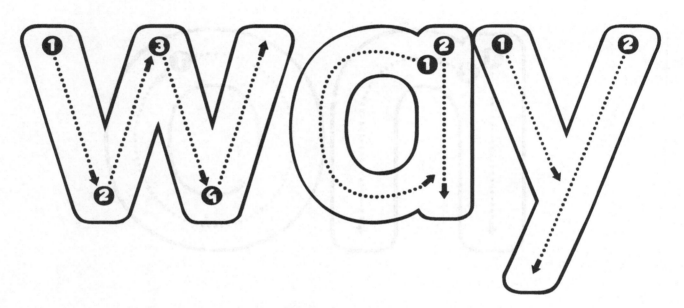

Trace the word until you are finished.

way way way

way way way

Write the word.

 **my**

Trace inside the big letters by following the numbers.

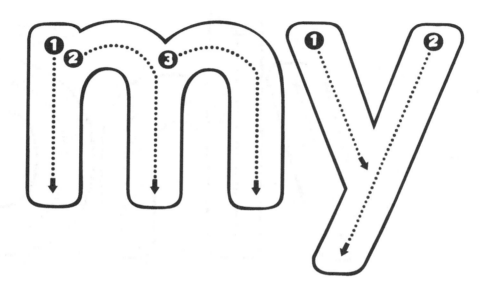

Trace the word until you are finished.

my my my my

my my my my

Write the word.

Trace inside the big letters by following the numbers.

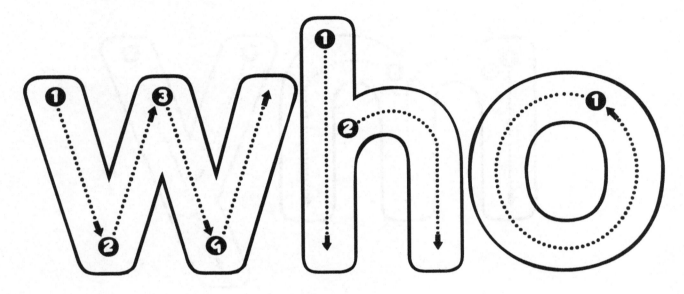

Trace the word until you are finished.

who who who

who who who

Write the word.

am

Trace inside the big letters by following the numbers.

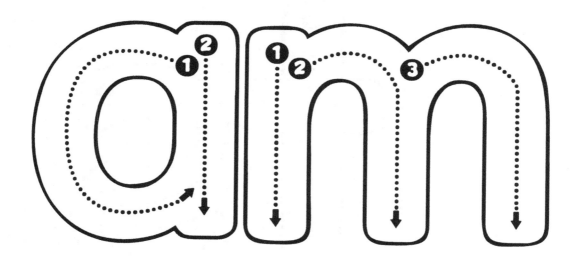

Trace the word until you are finished.

am am am am

am am am am

Write the word.

its

Name:................................

Trace inside the big letters by following the numbers.

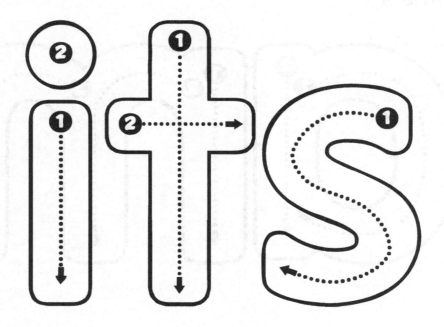

Trace the word until you are finished.

its   its   its   its

its   its   its   its

Write the word.

Trace inside the big letters by following the numbers.

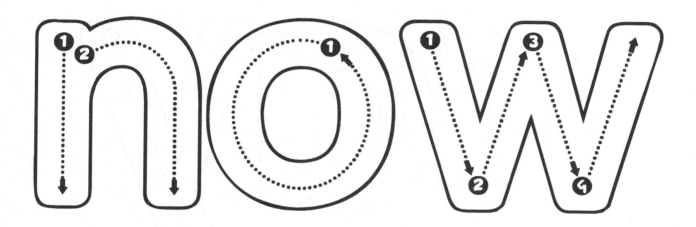

Trace the word until you are finished.

now now now

now now now

Write the word.

Trace inside the big letters by following the numbers.

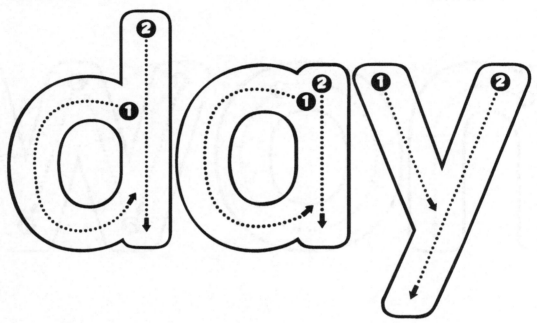

Trace the word until you are finished.

day day day day

day day day day

Write the word.

Trace inside the big letters by following the numbers.

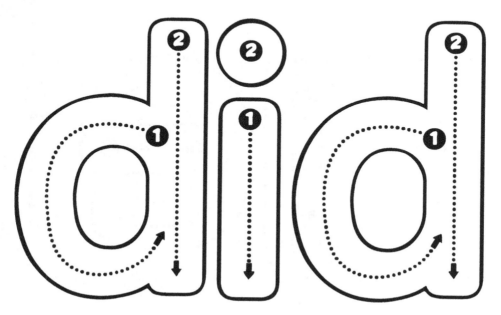

Trace the word until you are finished.

did did did did

did did did did

Write the word.

get

Trace inside the big letters by following the numbers.

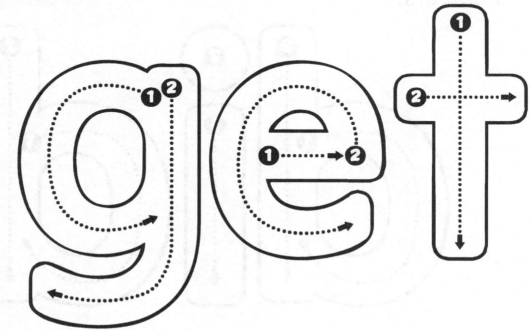

Trace the word until you are finished.

get get get get

get get get get

Write the word.

Trace inside the big letters by following the numbers.

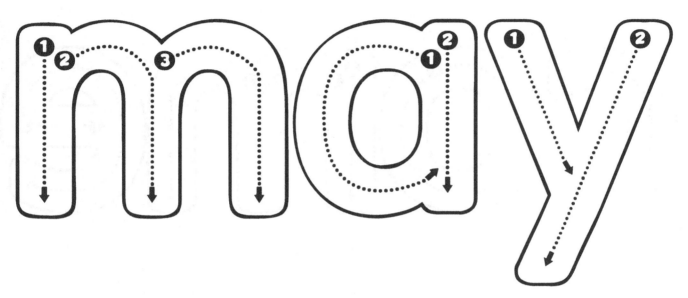

Trace the word until you are finished.

may   may   may

may   may   may

Write the word.

Trace inside the big letters by following the numbers.

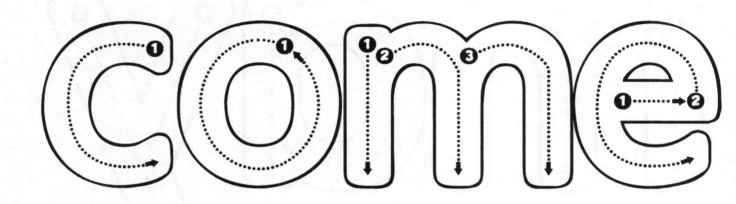

Trace the word until you are finished.

come   come   come

come   come   come

Write the word.

Name:.................................

will

Trace inside the big letters by following the numbers.

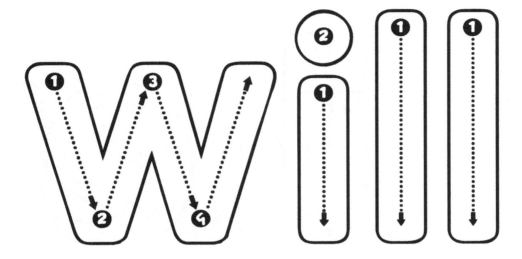

Trace the word until you are finished.

will will will will

will will will will

Write the word.

Trace inside the big letters by following the numbers.

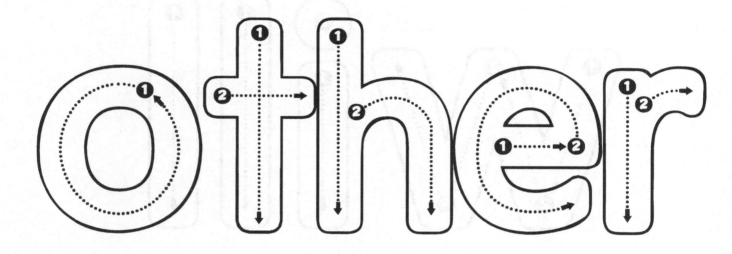

Trace the word until you are finished.

other other other

other other other

Write the word.

about

Trace inside the big letters by following the numbers.

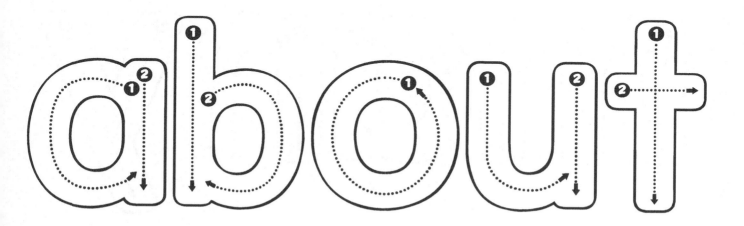

Trace the word until you are finished.

about about

about about

Write the word.

Trace inside the big letters by following the numbers.

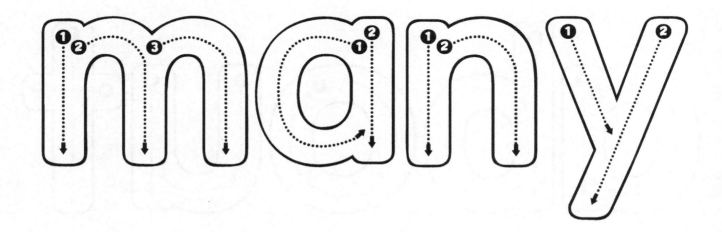

Trace the word until you are finished.

many many many

many many many

Write the word.

Trace inside the big letters by following the numbers.

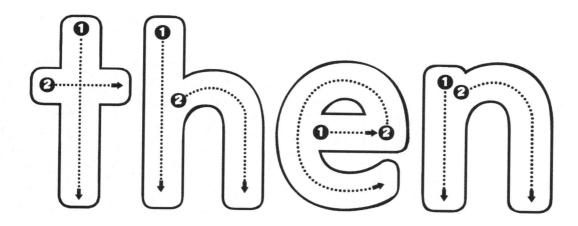

Trace the word until you are finished.

then then then

then then then

Write the word.

these

Trace inside the big letters by following the numbers.

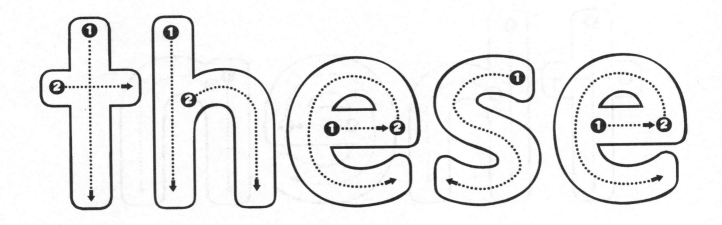

Trace the word until you are finished.

these these these

these these these

Write the word.

some

Trace inside the big letters by following the numbers.

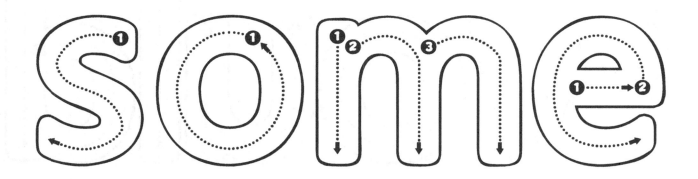

Trace the word until you are finished.

some some some

some some some

Write the word.

would

Trace inside the big letters by following the numbers.

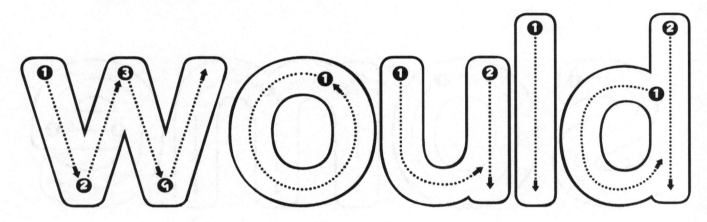

Trace the word until you are finished.

would would

would would

Write the word.

Trace inside the big letters by following the numbers.

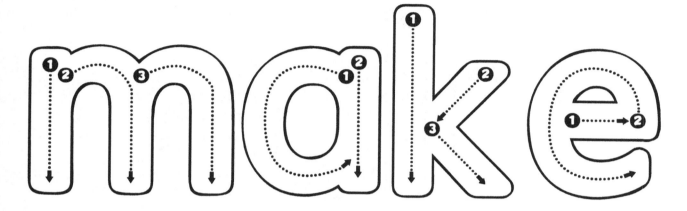

Trace the word until you are finished.

make make make

make make make

Write the word.

like

Trace inside the big letters by following the numbers.

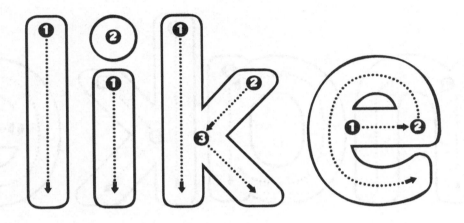

Trace the word until you are finished.

Write the word.

 **into**

Trace inside the big letters by following the numbers.

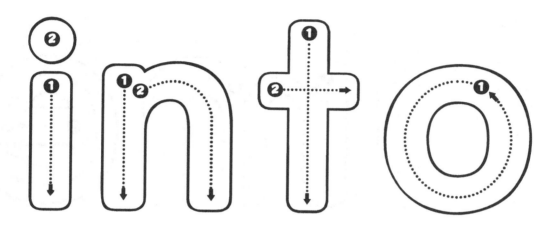

Trace the word until you are finished.

into into into into

into into into into

Write the word.

time

Trace inside the big letters by following the numbers.

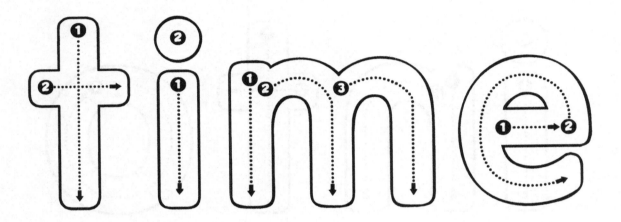

Trace the word until you are finished.

time time time

time time time

Write the word.

look

Trace inside the big letters by following the numbers.

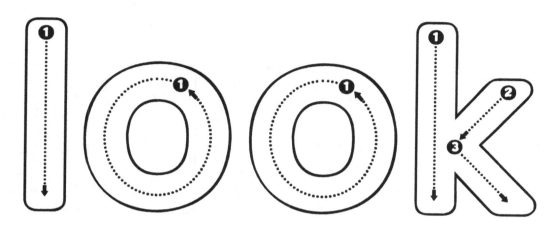

Trace the word until you are finished.

look look look

look look look

Write the word.

more

Trace inside the big letters by following the numbers.

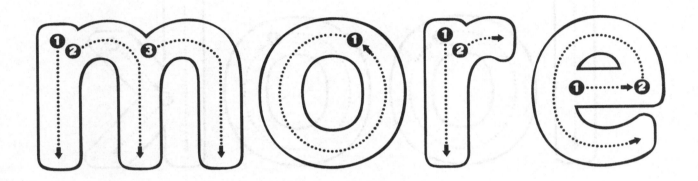

Trace the word until you are finished.

more more more

more more more

Write the word.

write

Trace inside the big letters by following the numbers.

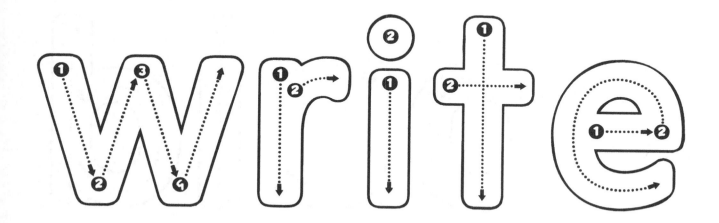

Trace the word until you are finished.

write write write

write write write

Write the word.

Trace inside the big letters by following the numbers.

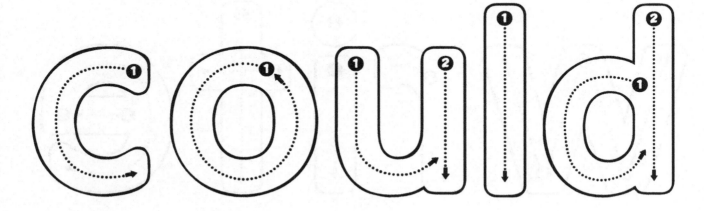

Trace the word until you are finished.

could could could

could could could

Write the word.

than

Trace inside the big letters by following the numbers.

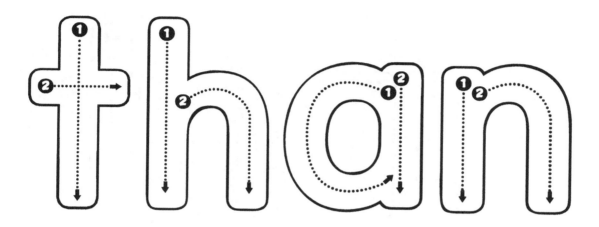

Trace the word until you are finished.

than than than

than than than

Write the word.

first

Trace inside the big letters by following the numbers.

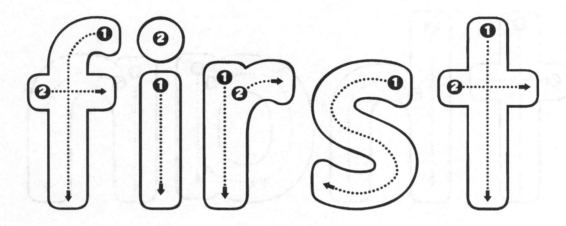

Trace the word until you are finished.

first first first

first first first

Write the word.

Trace inside the big letters by following the numbers.

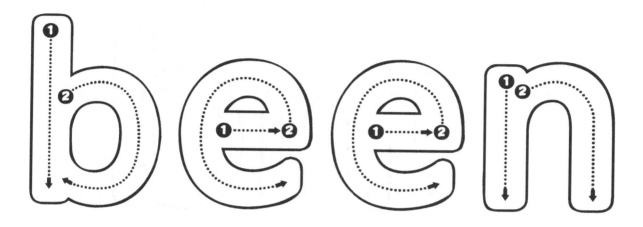

Trace the word until you are finished.

been been been

been been been

Write the word.

find

Trace inside the big letters by following the numbers.

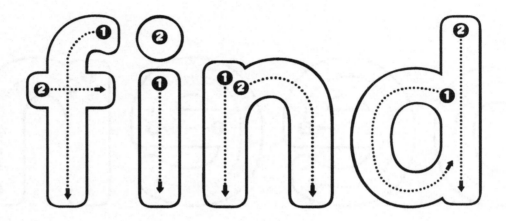

Trace the word until you are finished.

find find find

find find find

Write the word.

long

Trace inside the big letters by following the numbers.

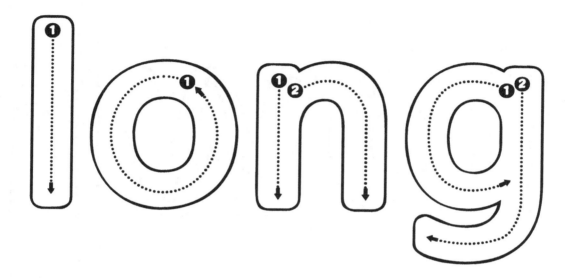

Trace the word until you are finished.

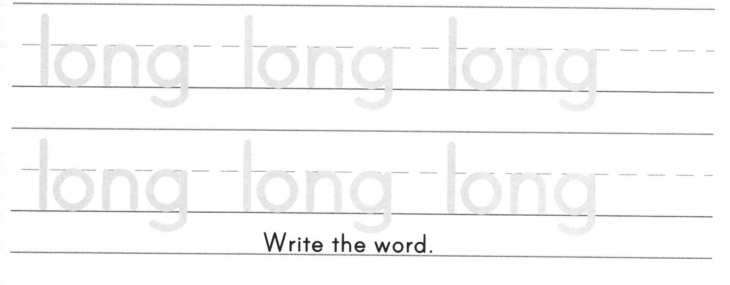

long long long

long long long

Write the word.

Trace inside the big letters by following the numbers.

Trace the word until you are finished.

down down down

down down down

Write the word.

Trace inside the big letters by following the numbers.

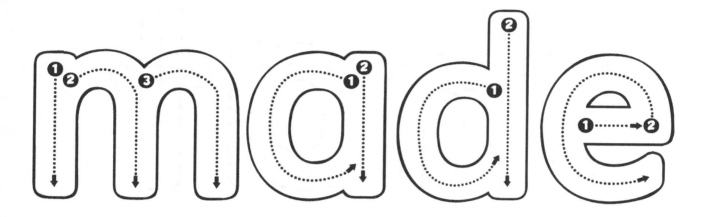

Trace the word until you are finished.

made   made   made

made   made   made

Write the word.

that

Trace inside the big letters by following the numbers.

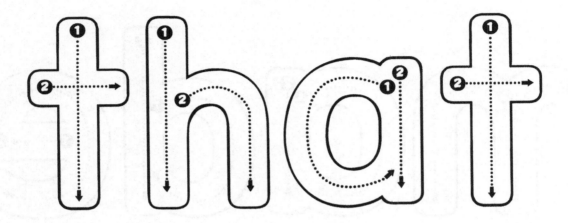

Trace the word until you are finished.

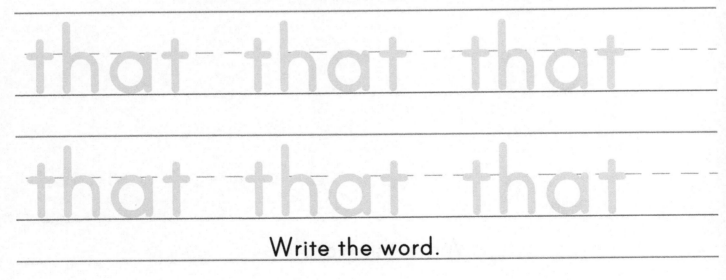

Write the word.

with

Name:...........................

Trace inside the big letters by following the numbers.

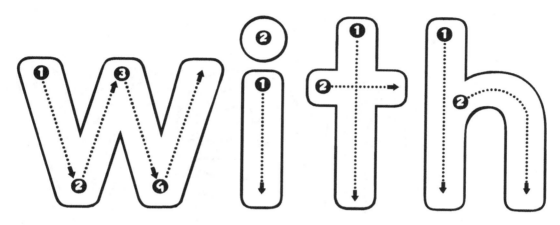

Trace the word until you are finished.

with with with

with with with

Write the word.

they

Trace inside the big letters by following the numbers.

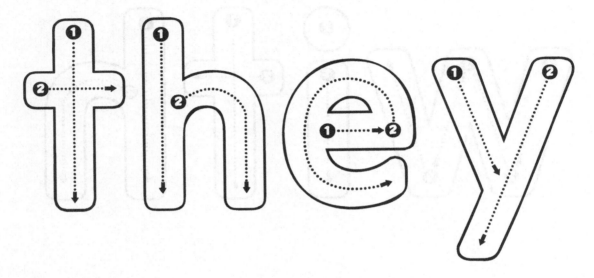

Trace the word until you are finished.

they they they

they they they

Write the word.

Trace inside the big letters by following the numbers.

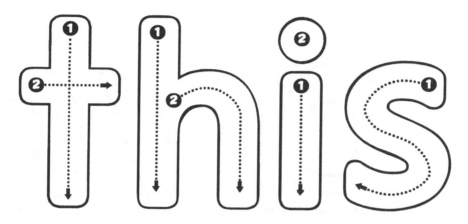

Trace the word until you are finished.

this this this

this this this

Write the word.

have

Trace inside the big letters by following the numbers.

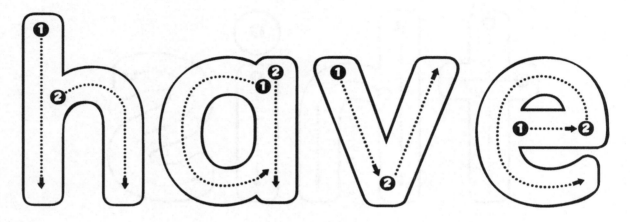

Trace the word until you are finished.

have   have   have

have   have   have

Write the word.

Trace inside the big letters by following the numbers.

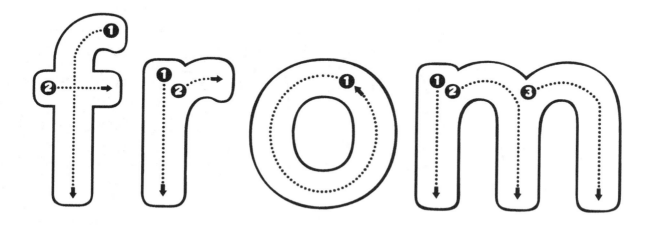

Trace the word until you are finished.

from from from

from from from

Write the word.

words

Trace inside the big letters by following the numbers.

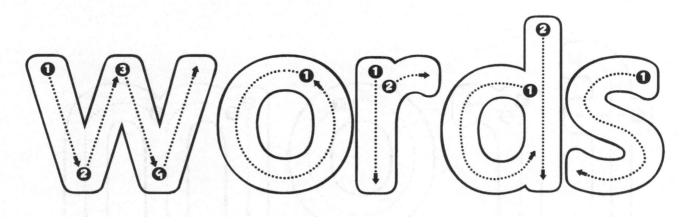

Trace the word until you are finished.

words words words

words words words

Write the word.

 **what**

Trace inside the big letters by following the numbers.

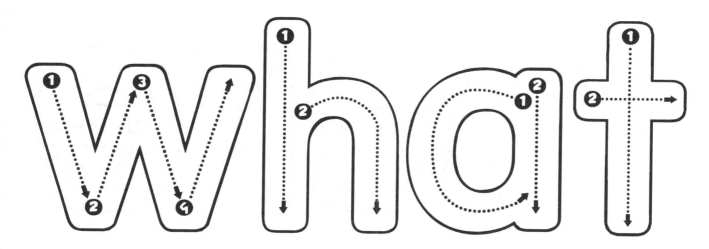

Trace the word until you are finished.

what what what

what what what

Write the word.

Trace inside the big letters by following the numbers.

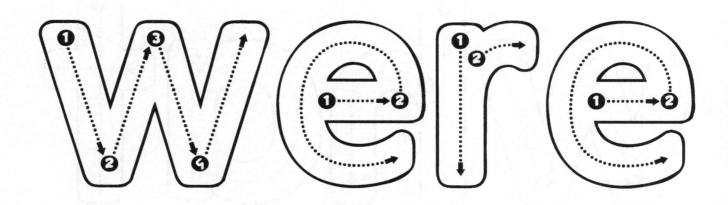

Trace the word until you are finished.

were were were

were were were

Write the word.

Trace inside the big letters by following the numbers.

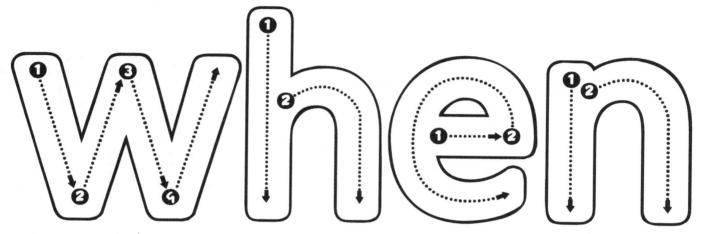

Trace the word until you are finished.

when when when

when when when

Write the word.

Trace inside the big letters by following the numbers.

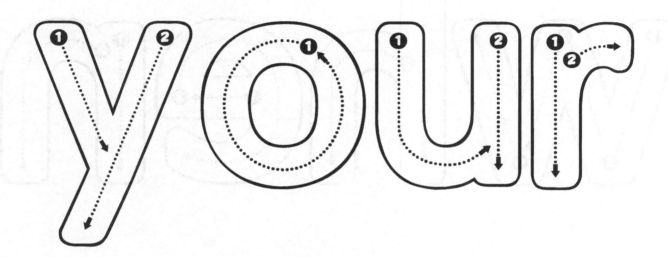

Trace the word until you are finished.

your your your

your your your

Write the word.

said

Trace inside the big letters by following the numbers.

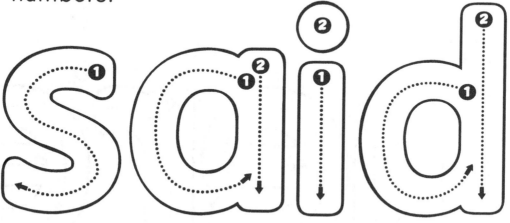

Trace the word until you are finished.

said   said   said

said   said   said

Write the word.

Trace inside the big letters by following the numbers.

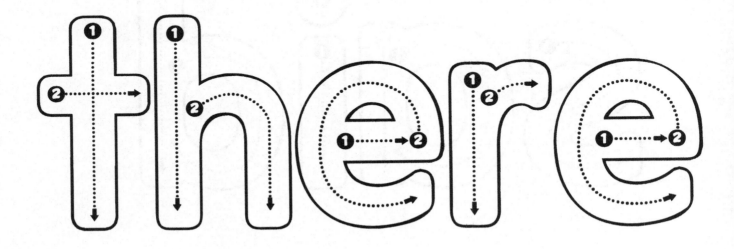

Trace the word until you are finished.

there there there

there there there

Write the word.

Trace inside the big letters by following the numbers.

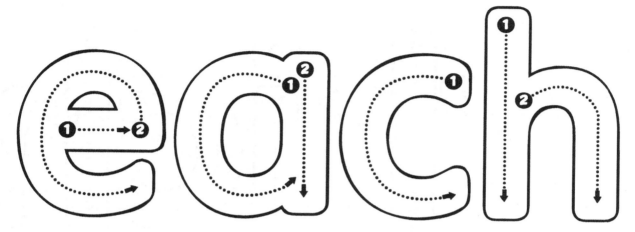

Trace the word until you are finished.

each   each   each

each   each   each

Write the word.

Trace inside the big letters by following the numbers.

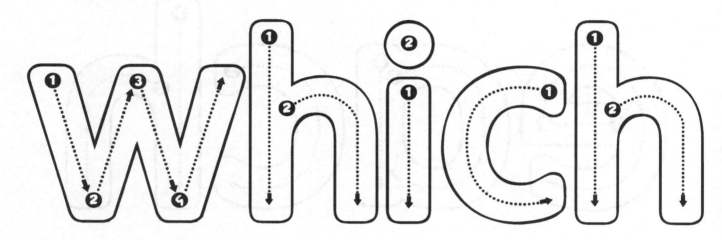

Trace the word until you are finished.

which which which

which which which

Write the word.

their

Trace inside the big letters by following the numbers.

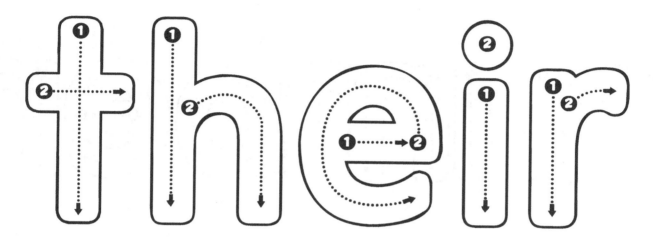

Trace the word until you are finished.

their their their

their their their

Write the word.

number

Trace inside the big letters by following the numbers.

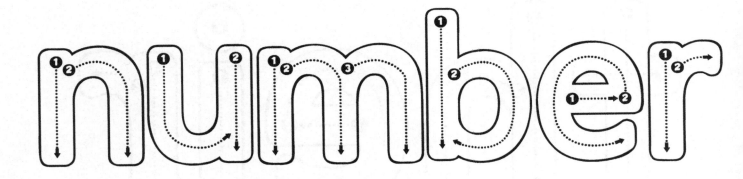

Trace the word until you are finished.

number number

number number

Write the word.

 **people**

Trace inside the big letters by following the numbers.

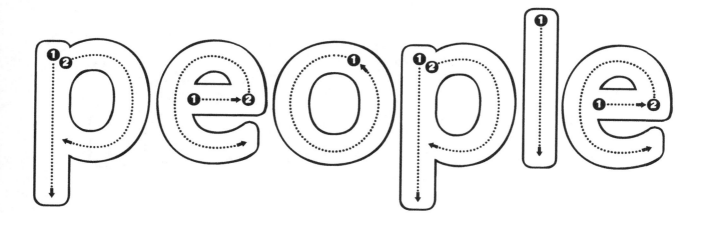

Trace the word until you are finished.

people people

people people

Write the word.

Trace inside the big letters by following the numbers.

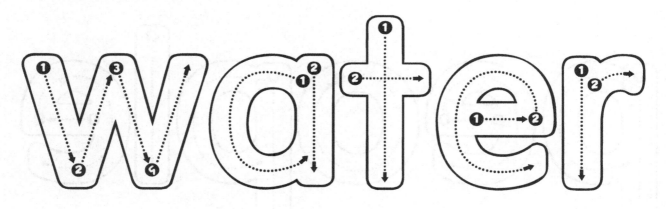

Trace the word until you are finished.

water water

water water

Write the word.

called

Trace inside the big letters by following the numbers.

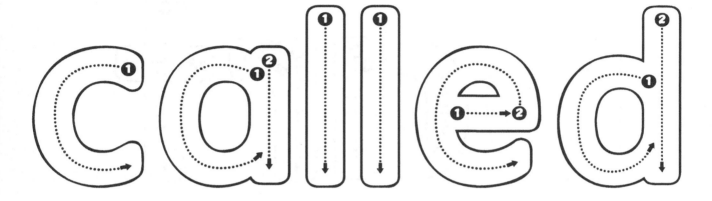

Trace the word until you are finished.

called called

called called

Write the word.

Trace inside the big letters by following the numbers.

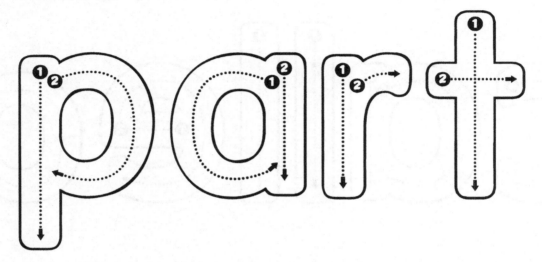

Trace the word until you are finished.

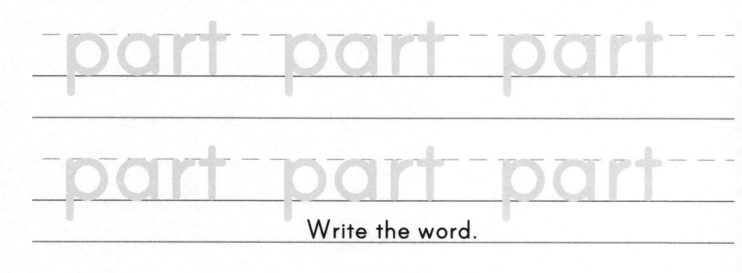

Write the word.

Made in the USA
Las Vegas, NV
17 October 2024

97023305R00057